FORTNITE BATTLE ROYALE HACKS

SURVIVING THE FINAL CIRCLE

FORTNITE BATTLE ROYALE HACKS

SURVIVING THE FINAL CIRCLE

AN UNOFFICIAL GUIDE TO TIPS AND TRICKS THAT OTHER GUIDES WON'T TEACH YOU

JASON R. RICH

Sky Pony Press
New York

TABLE OF CONTENTS

Section 1—The Inside Scoop on *Fortnite: Battle Royale* 1
- Prepare Yourself to Participate in Exciting Matches 2
- A Player's Top 10 Most Important Responsibilities During Each Match 3
- Discover the Different Game Play Modes. 10
- *Fortnite: Battle Royale* Is Continuously Evolving. 11
- During a Match, Everything You Do Leads Up to the End Game 16
- Listen Carefully to the Virtual World Around You 23

Section 2—Discover How to Safely Explore the Island. 27
- How to Read the Island Map 28
- Select Your Landing Destination Like a Pro 29

Section 3—Finding, Collecting, and Using Weapons & Loot Items 33
- What You Should Know About Weapons 33
- Three Tips to Improve Your Shooting Accuracy 34
- Understand How Weapons Are Rated and Categorized 36
- Choose Your Arsenal Wisely 39
- How and Where to Collect Ammo 41
- Finding, Collecting, and Using Loot Items 42
- Be on the Constant Lookout for Chests, Supply Drops, and Loot Llamas 43

Section 4— Collecting the Resources You'll Need
and Building Techniques 46
- Each Building Tile Has Its Own Strength. 46
- How to Become a Better Builder. 48
- Learn to Quickly Build "1x1" Fortresses. 53

Section 5—Survival Strategies and Fighting Tips. 57
  • Adapt Your Approach as Needed. 57

Section 6 —Welcome to the End Game: Survival and
Combat Strategies. 82
  • Preparing for the End Game. 82
  • Twelve End-Game Strategies to Get You Started 84
  • Additional End-Game Strategies 85

Section 7—*Fortnite: Battle Royale* Resources 95
  • Your *Fortnite: Battle Royale* Adventure Continues. 98

SECTION 1

THE INSIDE SCOOP ON *FORTNITE: BATTLE ROYALE*

What you're about to experience is a combat-oriented adventure that takes place on a mysterious island.

Fortnite: Battle Royale has become one of the most popular games in the world! Do you have what it takes to survive? You're about to put your gaming skills to the ultimate test.

Fortnite: Battle Royale can be experienced on a PC, Mac, Xbox One, PlayStation 4, Nintendo Switch, Apple iPhone, Apple iPad, or an Android-based mobile device. For the most part, the game is cross-platform compatible, so you can compete against other players who are using almost any popular gaming platform.

The actual game looks and sounds pretty much the same on all gaming systems. The location of certain information on the game screen, and which controller (or keyboard/mouse) buttons you need to press to accomplish specific tasks, will vary, however.

This unofficial strategy guide was created at the start of Season 5. The screenshots you see throughout this guide were taken using a PlayStation 4, Nintendo Switch, and iPad Pro. When you begin playing *Fortnite: Battle Royale*, you'll likely discover a bunch of new and exciting things have been added to the game, while certain other weapons and loot items may have been "vaulted."

Vaulted means something has been removed from the game, but Epic Games could re-introduce it in the future—like Jetpacks or Playground mode. Various labeled and unlabeled points of interest on the island may also have been added, changed, or eliminated altogether.

As you'll discover, *Fortnite: Battle Royale* can be played for free. However, optional in-game purchases (using real money) can be made in order to acquire a Battle Pass, purchase and unlock Battle Pass Tiers, or to acquire items that allow you to customize the appearance of your character.

Prepare Yourself to Participate in Exciting Matches

To become an awesome *Fortnite: Battle Royale* gamer, you'll need to master the ability to juggle multiple tasks and objectives during every match. Even if you know exactly what needs to be done, being successful will require practice . . . *a lot of practice*!

Your primary task—above all others—is to help defeat everyone else on the island—up to 99 enemy soldiers who also want to become the last person standing at the end of a match to achieve *#1 Victory Royale.*

A Player's Top 10 Most Important Responsibilities During Each Match

Your main objectives during each match include:

1. Safely explore the island.
2. Avoid the deadly storm.
3. Harvest and collect resources (wood, stone, and metal).
4. Find, collect, and manage a personal arsenal of weapons.
5. Locate and collect ammunition for your weapons.
6. Acquire and properly use loot items that can help a soldier survive.
7. Manage the inventory within your soldier's backpack (which only has six slots capable of holding weapons and/or loot items, in addition to the pickaxe).
8. Build ramps, bridges, structures, and fortresses using the collected resources in order to reach otherwise inaccessible places, or to provide defensive shielding during attacks.
9. Engage in combat against enemy soldiers in order to become the last person standing at the end of a match.
10. Prepare for the End Game of a match (also referred to as the Final Circle), when the eye of the storm is very small, and only a few enemy soldiers remain alive. This is when and where the fiercest battles typically take place.

While you're dealing with your enemies, it's also necessary to contend with a deadly storm. It will continuously shrink the amount of inhabitable land on the island. The storm continuously forces all surviving soldiers into a more confined fighting space. This is what it looks like when a soldier has been engulfed within the storm.

For every second a soldier remains within the storm, a portion of his or her Health meter (which is continuously displayed on the screen as a green bar) gets depleted slightly. As a match progresses, the amount of damage the storm causes per second increases. If a soldier's Health meter reaches zero while in the storm, he or she gets eliminated from the match. A soldier's Health meter starts at 100 and can't go any higher, but it will go down (sometimes quickly) when your soldier gets injured! There are a handful of loot items, like Apples, Med Kits, Bandages, and Chug Jugs, that can replenish your soldier's health during a match.

Displayed directly above the Health meter is a soldier's blue Shield meter. This starts off at zero. By collecting and using (or consuming) the right powerup loot items, it's possible to activate or replenish a soldier's shields up to a maximum level of 100. Shields do *not* protect against the storm or injuries resulting from a fall. They do, however, offer additional protection against weapon attacks and explosions.

At the start of a match, up to 100 soldiers (including the one you'll be controlling) travel via Battle Bus to the island, where everyone is dropped off.

Instead of landing on the island, soldiers are forced to leap from the Battle Bus and freefall down toward land. During this freefall, you're able to control the speed of descent and direction your soldier falls, so you can navigate to a specific landing destination.

If you plan to land at one of the island's most popular points of interest (locations), it's important to be one of the first soldiers to reach land, so you can quickly grab a weapon, take cover, and defend yourself. Otherwise, when you land, you could be shot and defeated within seconds. To increase your rate of descent during freefall, use your controller (or keyboard/mouse) to point your soldier downward. Here, the soldier was blown away seconds after landing on the clock tower in Tilted Towers. Another soldier beat him there and grabbed a weapon first.

To ensure your soldier lands safely on the island, his or her glider will automatically activate. When this happens, it slows down your soldier's rate of descent, and at the same time, gives you much more precise navigational control. It's possible to manually activate and deactivate the glider multiple times during freefall to better control your descent. As your soldier gets close to land, it automatically deploys.

Upon landing on the island, your soldier is armed with just a pickaxe. This can be used as a close-range weapon to fend off enemy soldiers, but it's no match against any type of gun or explosive. The pickaxe is mainly used to harvest resources (wood, stone, and metal), and to smash and clear away objects.

Your first two objectives once you land on the island are to find and grab your first weapon (and ammo), and to find cover, so you're not an easy target for enemies to attack.

While you're in the pre-deployment area (shown here) waiting to board the Battle Bus, or for a short time once you're flying aboard the bus, access the island map to discover the random route the bus will take over the island. While in the pre-deployment area, you can interact with other players, explore, and test out weapons. You can't be injured. Anything you collect will be left behind when you board the Battle Bus.

The random route the Battle Bus will take is temporarily displayed on the island map as a blue line, made up of arrows (shown here). Use this information to help you choose a landing spot, and if you're playing in Duos or Squads mode, for example, to mark your intended destination on the map for your squad mates to see.

Starting when you land on the island along with the up to 99 other soldiers, your primary goal is survival. You'll need to defeat your enemies or be defeated yourself. There's no second place. Each time your soldier gets defeated, he or she is immediately eliminated from the match and returned to the Lobby. Depending on how quickly soldiers are defeated, a match typically lasts approximately 15 minutes.

Discover the Different Game Play Modes

Fortnite: Battle Royale features three permanent game play modes—**Solo**, **Duos**, and **Squads**. Additional, but temporary, game play modes are offered from the Choose Game Mode screen, but these other modes change regularly. Choose one from the Lobby after launching the game.

The Solo game play mode allows you to experience a match on your own, against up to 99 other soldiers. Duos allows you to partner during a match with one online friend. Squads allows you to participate in a match with three squad mates, so the four of you can work together to achieve #1 Victory Royale against up to 96 enemy soldiers.

When playing Duos or Squads mode, for example, manually select who you'll be playing with using the game's Don't Fill feature. Choose the Fill feature, and the game will match you up with a random teammate or up to three squad mates. A continuous Internet connection is required to play *Fortnite: Battle Royale.*

Fortnite: Battle Royale Is Continuously Evolving

In order to keep *Fortnite: Battle Royale* fun, exciting, and challenging to play, and to ensure it never gets repetitive or boring, every week or two, Epic Games releases a game update (referred to as a *patch*). Each update makes minor tweaks to the game, and typically offers something new, such as a new type of weapon or loot item.

Every three months or so, Epic Games launches a new season of game play. In conjunction with each new season, the game gets a major update. This typically includes major changes to the island itself, along with new weapons, loot items, and challenges.

Because the game is continuously evolving, don't be surprised if you encounter something new or different as you explore the island and participate in matches.

Whenever something new is added to the game, or a change is made, a New Updates pop-up window or News screen appears when you launch the game. You can also learn more about what's new in the game by visiting: www.epicgames.com/fortnite/en-US/news.

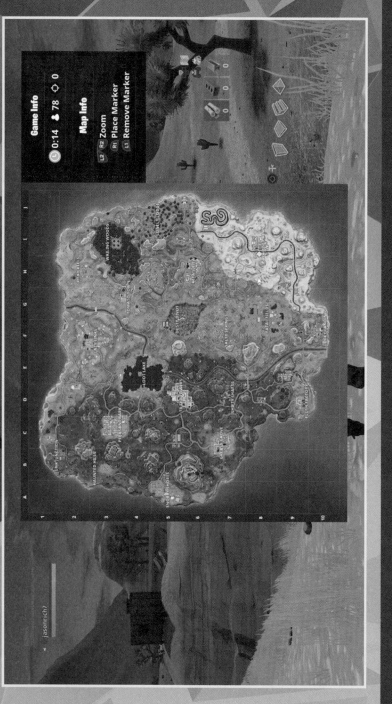

Every match takes place on the island. The island is divided up into about 20 major points of interest that are labeled and displayed on the island map. In addition to these labeled points of interest, many additional (but smaller) places to visit and explore can be found in between these labeled locations. This is how the island map looked at the start of Season 5.

If you're a veteran *Fortnite: Battle Royale* gamer, at the start of Season 5, you discovered that Moisty Mire (which was a swampy area of the island) was completely replaced by Paradise Palms (a desert area with several unique regions).

Another change to the island that happened at the start of Season 5 was that Anarchy Acres was replaced by Lazy Links (shown here), and pre-existing locations, like Dusty Divot and Risky Reels, received a makeover.

Atop one of the unlabeled mountains on the island (at map coordinates B5.5), you'll discover this Viking ship that can be explored. There's always a great selection of weapons, ammo, loot items, and other goodies to be found in this area.

There are many ways to travel around the island during a match. You can have your soldier walk or run, for example. He or she can also ride on a Shopping Cart or use a Bouncer (shown here) or Launch Pad to go airborne and then navigate in midair using the glider before landing. Periodically, Epic Games re-introduces Jetpacks that allow soldiers to travel in the air for limited amounts of time; however, Jetpacks are not always offered.

Stepping into a Rift will transport you up and away from your current location as you're exploring the island. A Rift-to-Go or Shockwave Grenade loot item can also be used for airborne travel.

Perhaps the most exciting and fun way to travel around the island is to ride in an All Terrain Kart (ATK). These souped-up golf carts can be driven along roads or paths, taken off-road, or can go airborne for a few seconds if driven over a ramp or cliff.

ATKs can be used by one player in Solo mode, or up to four team members can ride at once in Squads mode. In addition to performing tricky stunts while driving, the back of an ATK serves as a Launch Pad that a soldier can jump on.

During a Match, Everything You Do Leads Up to the End Game

There's a lot to do on the island, starting the moment your soldier safely lands at the desired location. However, everything you do during a match leads up to the End Game. Starting as soon as the soldiers have landed, the deadly storm begins to expand and move, making more and more of the island uninhabitable as a match goes on.

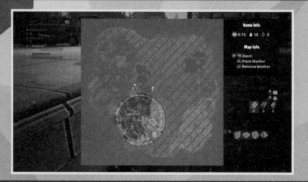

The storm's expansion forces the remaining enemy soldiers to continuously be pushed closer and closer together, until everyone who is still alive must engage in firefights if they have any hope of surviving. The areas of the island map that are displayed in pink on the map have already been decimated by the storm.

The outer circle that's displayed on the island map shows the eye of the storm, which is the area of the island that's still safe. The inner circle (when displayed) shows you where the storm will be expanding and moving to next.

The timer that's displayed below the Location Map on the main game screen counts down and tells you when the storm will be expanding and moving next. The white line that appears on both the island map and the Location Map displays the quickest route to follow in order to safely avoid the storm. Your current location on both maps is displayed as a small white triangle. If you're playing a Duos or Squads game, the location of your partner or squad mates is displayed as a red, yellow, blue, and/or purple triangle.

Anytime you're looking at the island map, you're able to zoom in to see a specific location in more detail.

While you're still in the pre-deployment area, aboard the Battle Bus, or at any time during a match, as you're viewing the island map, it's possible to place a colored marker. This marker is used to pinpoint a desired landing location or to set a meet-up point during a match.

After a marker is set, a colored flare is displayed. It can be seen from a distance (only by you and your team) as you explore the island. Each soldier is represented by a different colored flare. If you're playing a Duos or Squads game, each player should mark their intended landing location while still in the pre-deployment area, so everyone can meet up at the same location, if that's the strategy your team decides to adopt.

In addition to gathering a personal weapon arsenal along with a few loot items that get stored in your backpack, one of the tasks you'll definitely want to focus on throughout each match is collecting resources (wood, stone, and metal). These resources are used for building. Here, the soldier is harvesting wood by smashing a tree with her pickaxe.

During the final few minutes of each match, the storm will have ravaged most of the island, leaving just a small circle of space that's inhabitable. This is referred to as the Final Circle. It's here that the remaining soldiers are forced to fight each other, so that one soldier (or one team/squad) will emerge as the winner. Here, one soldier just shot a Rocket Launcher at an enemy's wooden fortress in front of him. The explosion is in the process of blowing up and destroying the fortress (with the enemy soldier still inside).

To survive the Final Circle will require you to equip your soldier with the most powerful weapons, explosives, and projectile weapons available. You'll also need to go into the End Game having harvested and collected a hefty collection of resources (up to 1,000 wood, 1,000 stone, and 1,000 metal), so that you're able to build fortresses and ramps as they're needed. Rocket Launchers, Grenade Launchers, and Guided Missile Launchers will destroy most structures, as well as defeat anyone hiding inside them.

One of the great things about *Fortnite: Battle Royale* is that because you're competing against up to 99 other gamers, who are controlling their respective soldiers in real-time, no two matches are ever the same. Thus, you'll need to adopt your End Game strategy based on the challenges you encounter during each specific match.

Sometimes, you'll be required to build an elaborate and sturdy fortress within the Final Circle, so you can attack enemies using projectile explosive weapons and long-range sniper rifles (equipped with a scope), for example. Shown here is a 1x1 fortress that's four levels tall. The bottom level is made from stone, so it offers a stronger foundation. The soldier in the opposite fortress during this End Game is using the scope of his rifle to spy on the enemy and determine the best strategy to launch an attack.

Depending on the random location on the island where the End Game takes place, as well as the strategies you see your adversaries using, instead of focusing on fortress building and launching attacks from a fortress, you may discover it's necessary to engage in close-range combat with your final enemies. In this case, it's important to arm yourself with the most powerful guns available to you that work well at close- to mid-range.

Throughout each match, if you're able to survive until the End Game, it's important to collect as much ammunition as possible, so you'll be able to use the weapons in your arsenal.

You can gather ammo by either opening an Ammo Box (shown here) or by collecting batches of ammo you find lying on the ground. Grab all ammo you're able to, even if it's for weapons you don't currently have in your possession. If you don't have enough of the right type of ammo when you need it, your weapons will be rendered useless.

Listen Carefully to the Virtual World Around You

Every point of interest on the island offers a unique virtual location within which you can explore, engage in firefights, build, and if you choose, destroy.

Using your pickaxe, you can smash just about anything. Based on what the item or structure is made of, at the same time you destroy something, you'll harvest wood, stone, or metal. Doing this will generate noise that your nearby enemies will hear.

Guns and explosive weapons can also be used to destroy almost any-thing found on the island, including obstacles that are in your way, or entire structures. When you shoot at or blow up something, this gets rid of it, but you won't collect or harvest any resources. Doing this will also generate sound that could give away your position. On the left is what a gas station looked like before it was blown up using three Grenades.

After tossing three Grenades and allowing them to detonate seconds later, the entire inside of the gas station was gutted and everything inside was destroyed, including the back wall. If you look carefully at the screenshot on the right, you can now see the grassy hill through the window. If an enemy were hiding in this gas station when the Grenades detonated, he'd be toast. The outer structure of the gas station sur-vived, because it was made of stone, as opposed to wood.

Just about anything you do on the island generates noise, whether you're walking around or running, smashing objects, harvesting resources, building, opening/closing doors, or driving an ATK. All of your adversaries will also generate sounds that can be heard by others who are nearby.

Based on your actions, you can easily give away your current location if you make too much noise. If you run toward an opponent, even if he can't see you right away, he'll often hear your footsteps as you get closer.

To make your experience on the island more realistic, you'll also hear ambient sounds all around you, based on where you are and what you're doing. Chests make a unique sound that you can hear when you're close to one, even if it's hidden behind a wall or object. The storm also makes a unique noise as it's approaching.

Always pay attention to the sounds you're hearing, as they can alert you of impending danger. The best way to hear the sound effects in the game, the way they were meant to be heard, is to connect a wireless or wired gaming headset (with a built-in microphone) to your gaming system. At the very least, use stereo headphones when playing *Fortnite: Battle Royale*. Turtle Beach Corp. (www.turtlebeach.com) is just one of many companies that offer high-quality gaming headsets with a built-in microphone.

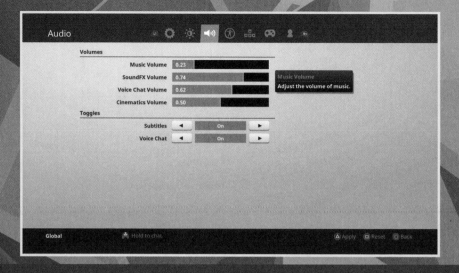

To ensure you hear all of the game's sound effects clearly, from the Lobby screen, access the Game Menu (it has a gear-shaped icon), and then access the Audio sub-menu (shown here). You'll likely find it useful to turn down the Music Volume and Cinematics Volume options. Turn up the Sound FX Volume slider. If you have a gaming headset (with a microphone), also turn up the Voice Chat Volume option.

If you're a noob (beginner), leave all of the other menu options at their default settings until you've gained experience playing *Fortnite: Battle Royale* and desire to tweak specific settings to enhance certain in-game features, based on your personal game play style and preferences.

SECTION 2

DISCOVER HOW TO SAFELY EXPLORE THE ISLAND

The island offers approximately 20 labeled points of interest on the map, along with many unlabeled, smaller, but equally interesting places to explore and engage in battles. Each location offers a different type of terrain, which if you're smart, you'll learn to use to your advantage.

As you travel between points of interest and plan routes to avoid the storm, you'll stumble upon individual structures, or sometimes a group of structures. These structures are often worth visiting, because inside, you'll sometimes find weapons, ammo, and loot items, or maybe even a chest. Many of these structures also provide a secure place to use health and shield powerups to restore your Health and Shield meters. This RV park, for example, is located at map coordinates I5.5, but it's not labeled on the map.

It's important that you discover how and when to access the island map, and that you learn how to identify key locations.

While you're in the pre-deployment area waiting to board the Battle Bus, or while the Battle Bus is in the air, access the island map. A blue line (comprised of arrows) displays the random route the Battle Bus will take over the island, so you can more easily decide when to leave the bus and choose a preferred landing site.

Do you want to land in a less popular and more secluded area, so you can gather weapons and resources, or would you prefer to drop down into a popular part of the island, where you're virtually guaranteed to encounter enemy soldiers and be forced to fight almost immediately?

Suppose your desired landing spot is Flush Factory (located between map coordinates C9.5 and D9.5), but when you look at the island map that shows the route the Battle Bus will take, its route takes you nowhere near this area. As with all points of interest, even if the route the Battle Bus takes does not travel directly over your desired land-ing location, you can travel during free fall more than halfway across the entire island before your soldier's glider automatically deploys. As a result, you can almost always reach any area on the map.

How to Read the Island Map

The full island map is divided into quadrants (boxes). Displayed along the top margin of the map (from left to right) are the letters "A" through "J." Along the left margin of the map, from top to bottom, are the numbers

"1" through "10." Using these letters and numbers, you can easily identify any location or quadrant on the map.

For example, quadrant E2.5 on the map corresponds with Lazy Links, while coordinates H6 corresponds with Retail Row. Lucky Landing can be found between coordinates F10 and G10. The Viking ship can be found on an unlabeled mountain, near map coordinates B5.5.

Select Your Landing Destination Like a Pro

If you're landing in or near any point of interest (or known structure), land directly on a house, building, or structure's roof. Sometimes, you'll find weapons, ammo, or loot to collect out in the open, lying on the roof. Upon landing, smash through the roof to the attic of a house, or the top floor of a building or tower. You'll often find a chest in these high-up areas, so you can quickly arm yourself before encountering enemy soldiers.

When you watch live streams (on YouTube or Twitch.tv) of the top-ranked *Fortnite: Battle Royale* players, one strategy you'll often see them implement is choosing a very remote place to land once their soldier jumps from the Battle Bus. They'll choose a landing location they know offers multiple chests that can be found and opened within moments of landing.

One ideal landing location for this strategy is between map coordinates I2.5 and J2.5 (outside of Wailing Woods). Land on top of this house that contains a tall wooden tower on top of it. Smash your way downward using the pickaxe.

After you've collected an initial arsenal of weapons and loot items, instead of spending time visiting the island's various points of interest, determine where the storm is headed (by looking at the map), and avoid enemy soldiers early on in a match by staying exclusively in the outskirts of popular island locations. This shed, located at map coordinates E3, is in the outskirts of Lazy Links, for example. Inside, you may find a chest, or at least weapons and ammo on the ground.

By staying out of the popular points of interest early in the match, you'll likely encounter only a few enemy soldiers. You can choose to fight them, or often avoid them altogether to ensure your soldier will stay alive longer. As the storm continues to expand, focus on staying within the eye of the storm (the circle), while building up your arsenal and resource collection before the circle gets really small, and you're forced to fight the remaining enemy soldiers during the End Game.

Among the many other potential landing sites that allow you to quickly grab weapons, ammo, and loot items, but often avoid immediate enemy contact, includes a cluster of homes and buildings near map coordinates D8, and the tall wooden tower located between map coordinates I4.5 and J4.5 (outside of Lonely Lodge). Up to three chests can often be found within this tower.

If you take a more aggressive approach and land in the heart of a point of interest, like Tilted Towers, Paradise Palms, or Lazy Links, you will definitely encounter enemies, often within the first few seconds after landing. Initially, you'll only be armed with a pickaxe, which is no match for any type of gun or explosive. Here, a soldier just landed on a rooftop of a building in Tilted Towers. Unfortunately, he wasn't alone and was not the first soldier to grab a weapon.

If another soldier has beaten you to your landing location, chances are he or she will already be armed with a weapon and you'll be virtually defenseless. Unless you quickly find cover or a weapon, you will be eliminated from the match within seconds of landing.

SECTION 3

FINDING, COLLECTING, AND USING WEAPONS & LOOT ITEMS

Available throughout the island are hundreds of different types of weapons. The trick is to find and collect the best weapons (and related ammunition) that'll help you survive and defeat your enemies.

What You Should Know About Weapons

The weapon categories firearms and explosives typically fall into include: Assault Rifles, Grenade Launchers, Grenades, Miniguns, Pistols, Rocket Launchers, Shotguns, SMGs (Sub Machine Guns), and Sniper Rifles. Other types of weapons are always being introduced into the game.

Many *Fortnite: Battle Royale* gamers agree that the most useful weapon to master is any type of shotgun. There are several types of shotguns to be found within the game. They can be used in close-range or mid-range combat situations, or even at a distance. (From a distance, they're harder to aim accurately than a rifle with a scope, for example.) When using a shotgun, always try for a headshot to inflict the most damage.

Each category of weapon can be used for a different purpose. Based on the type of enemy encounter you're experiencing at any given moment, it's essential that you choose the most appropriate and powerful weapon at your disposal.

Three Tips to Improve Your Shooting Accuracy

Regardless of which weapon you're using, your aim improves when you crouch down and you press the Aim button for the weapon you're using. When you press the Aim button before the trigger button, you'll zoom in a bit on your opponent, and you'll have more precise control over the positioning of the targeting crosshairs.

While it's often necessary to be running or jumping at the same time that you're firing a weapon, your accuracy improves when you're standing still. It improves even more by pressing the Aim button before pressing the trigger button. As this End Game approaches, there's an enemy fortress off in the distance (in the center of the screen). This soldier stood still and aimed a Rocket Launcher at his target.

It's a wooden fortress, so one direct hit from a Rocket Launcher's ammo, at a vulnerable spot in the fortress, led to its quick destruction.

You almost always have an advantage when you're higher up than your opponent and shooting in a downward direction.

A Thermal Scoped Assault Rifle will come in handy anytime during a match for spying on your enemies from a distance. However, you should conserve your ammo for this weapon until the End Game.

Early on in a match, use this weapon as a fancy set of binoculars. It allows you to see through walls and spot hiding enemies. The yellow figure near the center of the crosshairs is an enemy soldier who is running in the distance.

Understand How Weapons Are Rated and Categorized

While every weapon has the ability to cause damage and potentially defeat your adversaries, each is rated based on several criteria, including its rarity. Weapons are color coded with a hue around them to showcase their rarity.

Weapons with a **gray** hue are "Common."

Weapon with a **green** hue are "Uncommon."

Weapons with a **blue** hue are "Rare."

Weapons with a **purple** hue are "Epic."

"Legendary" weapons (with an **orange** hue) are hard to find, extra powerful, and very rare. If you're able to obtain one, grab it!

It is possible to collect several of the same weapon, but each could have a different rarity. So, if you collect two of the same weapon, and one is rare, but the second is legendary, definitely keep the legendary weapon and trade the other for something else when you find a replacement.

If you're really interested in how a weapon is rated, evaluate its DPR (Damage Per Second) rating, overall Damage Rating, Fire Rate, MAG (Magazine) Capacity, and Reload Time. This is information that Epic Games tweaks often. Select a weapon when viewing your Backpack Inventory screen to see details about it.

There are also plenty of websites, including: IGN.com (www.ign. com/wikis/fortnite/Weapons), Gameskinny.com (www.gameskinny. com/9mt22/complete-fortnite-battle-royale-weapons-stats-list), and RankedBoost.com (https://rankedboost.com/fortnite/best-weapons-tier-list), that provide the current stats for each weapon offered in *Fortnite: Battle Royale*, based on the latest tweaks made to the game. Just make sure when you look at this information online, it refers to the most recently released version of *Fortnite: Battle Royale*.

Choose Your Arsenal Wisely

Based on where you are, what challenges you're currently encountering, and what you anticipate your needs will be, stock your backpack with the weapons and tools you believe you'll need. Don't forget, you also need to stockpile appropriate weapons, ammo, loot items, and resources prior to the End Game.

At any time, your soldier's backpack can hold six items (including the pickaxe). That leaves five slots in which you can carry different types of guns, alternative weapons (such as Remote Explosives or Grenades), and/or powerup loot items (such as Med Kits, Chug Jugs, Shield Potions, Bandages, or Slurp Juice). Make smart inventory decisions throughout each match. What a soldier is currently carrying is shown here in the bottom-right side of the screen. The location where this information is displayed will vary based on which gaming system you're using.

During a match, check your Backpack Inventory screen to learn more about each of the weapons you're carrying, and to determine how much of each type of ammunition you have on hand. To do this, access the Backpack Inventory screen and then highlight and select a weapon. Here, a Suppressed Pistol is selected and information about it is shown. From this screen, it's also possible to re-organize the backpack's contents, so it becomes faster and easier to grab the weapons or items you tend to use the most frequently. You're also able to drop weapons or items you no longer want.

The various types of ammunition you've collected, how much of each ammo type you have on hand, and which weapons each ammo type can be used with is also displayed on the Backpack Inventory screen. While viewing this screen, select a specific ammunition type to learn more about it. Here, below the Ammo heading on the right side of the screen, the Ammo: Shells icon is selected. From the left side of the screen, you'll learn that this type of ammo is used in shotguns, and that this soldier currently has four of the shells on hand.

Some weapons, like pistols, are ideal for close-range firefights. Other weapons (like shotguns) are better suited for mid-range combat. Rifles with a scope and the more powerful, projectile explosive weapons (like Rocket Launchers) are ideal for destroying structures and/or enemies from a distance. It's important to find and carry an assortment of weapons, so you're able to deal with any fighting situation you encounter.

Based on the location you're in, you can anticipate many of your weapon needs. For example, if you'll be fighting within homes, buildings, or structures, weapons best suited for close-range combat (and related ammo), such as some type of pistol or shotgun, will be needed.

How and Where to Collect Ammo

Without having the appropriate ammunition on hand, whatever weapons you're carrying will be useless. Throughout each match, there are several ways to find and collect ammo, including:

- It can sometimes be found out in the open, lying on the ground.
- It can be collected from enemies you defeat.
- It's offered within chests, Supply Drops, and Loot Llamas.
- It's offered within Ammo Boxes.

Finding, Collecting, and Using Loot Items

There are many types of loot items available to you during a match. Some are very rare, while others can be collected often. Each type of loot item serves one of four purposes.

- **Weapons**—Traps, Grenades, Stink Bombs, Impulse Grenades, and Remote Explosives are collected and then used against enemies when needed. Some of these items require an inventory slot within your backpack. Others, like Traps, get stored along with your resources. In most cases, you can carry multiples of the same item, such as three or six Grenades, within the same Backpack Inventory slot.
- **Tools**—Items like a Port-A-Fort or Bush can be useful to aid in your survival.
- **Health and/or Shield Powerups**—Med Kits, Chug Jugs, Bandages, Shield Potions, and Slurp Juice can be used to replenish your Health meter and/or activate and then replenish your Shield meter. Each of these items takes time to consume or use, during which time your soldier will be vulnerable to attack.
- **Transportation**—Shopping Carts, Bouncers, Launch Pads, Rifts, and All Terrain Karts are examples of items and in-game phenomenon that can randomly be found throughout the island and that will help you travel around.

Most loot items can be found within chests, Supply Drops, and Loot Llamas, as well as lying out in the open (often on the ground). Many of these items can also be acquired after you defeat an enemy—when he or she drops everything they were carrying as they're being eliminated from the match. Some items can be obtained from Vending Machines (by exchanging resources you've collected within the game).

Be on the Constant Lookout for Chests, Supply Drops, and Loot Llamas

One of your first priorities once you (and your teammates) land on the island is to find weapons.

Some weapons and ammo can be found lying out in the open (on the ground).

Throughout the island—mainly within buildings, homes, and other structures, as well as inside of trucks, but sometimes out in the open— you'll discover chests.

Chests have a golden glow and make a sound when you get close to them. Open chests to collect a random selection of weapons, ammo, loot items, and resources. To collect a chest's contents, you must be the first soldier to open it during a match.

Some chests are usually found at the same spot on the map match after match, although this is changing as Epic Games releases new game updates. Sometimes, chests randomly appear during each match, so always be on the lookout for them (and listen carefully for the sound they make).

As you're exploring various areas, listen closely for the unique sound chests emit. You'll often hear this sound before a chest comes into view. Assuming it's safe, approach the chest and open it. Then be ready to grab the items you want or need. Anytime you're searching a home, you'll often find one or more chests in an attic, basement, or garage. Sometimes, they're just sitting out in the open.

At random times during a match, you may be lucky enough to spot a Supply Drop. This is a floating balloon with a wooden crate attached. They're somewhat rare. If you spot one, approach with caution, and open the crate. Inside you'll discover a random selection of weapons, loot items, ammo, and resource icons.

An even rarer object to come across on the island is a Loot Llama. This colorful item looks like a piñata. Smash it open and you'll discover a collection of random weapons, ammo, loot items, and resource icons. Typically, the weapons found within Loot Llamas are rare and often "legendary."

Instead of opening a Loot Llama, an alternate strategy is to place remote explosives on or near it and then hide. As soon as an enemy soldier approaches, manually detonate the explosives to defeat the enemy. As you approach a Supply Drop or Loot Llama, consider quickly building walls around yourself and the object, so you're protected before opening the crate or smashing the Loot Llama.

SECTION 4

COLLECTING THE RESOURCES YOU'LL NEED AND BUILDING TECHNIQUES

Becoming an expert builder, especially in the heat of battle, requires practice, as well as some creativity when it comes to designing structures. Either by watching live streams of expert players on YouTube or Twitch.tv, or by staying in Spectator mode once you're eliminated from a match, watch the final stages of matches carefully to learn the best techniques for building fortresses.

To practice your building technique, travel to an unpopular and unpopulated area of the island, focus on collecting resources, and then fine tune your building skills. Experiment with different structure designs, and develop the skillset needed to be able to build very quickly, without having to think too much about it. If the Playground game play mode is currently offered (it's added and removed from the game periodically), this is the perfect place to practice building.

Each Building Tile Has Its Own Strength

There are four shapes of building tiles—vertical wall tiles, horizontal floor/ceiling tiles, ramp/stair tiles, and pyramid-shaped tiles. Once you enter into Building mode, first choose your building material. Next, choose where you want to build. Finally, one at a time, select which building tile you want to use.

Once it's been fully built, each tile has an HP level that determines how much damage it can withstand before collapsing or being destroyed. During the building process, a tile's HP increases gradually. Wood is the fastest to build with, while working with stone is slightly slower. Metal takes the longest to build with but offers the most protection.

Each tile costs 10 of the selected resource to build. Remember, when you're in Building mode, you can't use a weapon. You'll definitely need to practice quickly switching between Combat mode and Building mode.

Here's a list of the HP strength offered by each tile type once its fully built. Keep in mind, this information could change slightly if Epic Games tweaks this aspect of the game.

TILE SHAPE	WOOD	STONE	METAL
Horizontal Floor/Ceiling Tile	140 HP	280 HP	460 HP
Vertical Wall Tile	150 HP	300 HP	500 HP
Ramp/Stairs Tile	140 HP	280 HP	460 HP
Pyramid-Shaped Tile	140 HP	280 HP	460 HP

When you go into Edit mode to alter a tile, by adding a door or window, for example, the strength of that tile changes. Each tile has its own HP meter that is displayed when you face the tile.

How to Become a Better Builder

The trick to becoming a highly skilled builder is speed. Achieving speed takes practice! Here are some additional strategies to help you become an expert builder.

When building a fortress, cover all sides. Don't forget to build a roof to protect you from assaults from above. Stone was used here.

A basic fort can consist of four walls around you. If the ground you're building on isn't level, add a floor tile and then build on top of it. To protect yourself from attacks from above, build a flat ceiling tile as a roof, and for added protection, build a pyramid-shaped tile on top of that.

As you're building the foundation or a fortress, for example, reinforce the first floor using metal. Then, if an enemy manages to sneak up and launch a close-range attack, you'll have extra time to react before your fortress crumbles.

Aside from using a Rocket Launcher from a distance to destroy part of or an entire enemy fortress, most types of mid to long-range shotguns and rifles will work. However, if you can sneak up on the enemy from the ground, you can attach a Remote Explosive to the base of their fort or toss a few Grenades. This is typically quicker than continuously shooting at a fortress wall to weaken or destroy it. Here, three Remote Explosives were placed near the closed door of this small fortress. Once activated, the Remote Explosives have a flashing blue light.

With one big blast, the fortress was destroyed.

Building an Over-Under Ramp uses twice the resources but allows you to travel up higher (or go down from someplace high up), while protecting yourself from attacks originating from above you. As you're building a ramp, position the building cursor in the middle of the upper and lower tiles to build both at the same time.

When you need quick protection, build a vertical wall with the strongest material you have available, and then quickly build a ramp (or stairs) directly behind it. Crouch down behind this structure for protection. Doing this provides a double layer of shielding that an enemy will have to shoot through or destroy in order to reach you. Plus, by crouching down, you become a smaller target.

This is the same structure (one vertical wall with a ramp behind it), but with vertical walls built on both sides to provide extra protection from flank attacks.

In some cases, building two ramps side-by-side gives you an advantage. An opponent who's below you can't see your exact location when you move back and forth between ramps. Also, if one ramp is about to get destroyed, quickly leap to the other to survive the attack. Yes, this requires more resources, but it's often worth it.

A "ramp rush" is a strategy that involves building a tall ramp quickly, so you're able to move directly toward and over an enemy (or their base) to initiate an attack. This strategy is commonly used during an End Game when attacking an enemy holed up in their own fortress.

Smashing wooden pallets often generates more wood than smashing trees. However, trees provide more wood than smashing the walls, floors, and ceilings of houses or buildings. Giant trees, like those found in Wailing Woods, tend to generate the most wood. During normal combat, wood is typically the best resources to use. Save your stone and metal for fort building during the End Game.

Harvesting metal from cars, RVs, cargo containers, and trucks, for example, generates the best results, but also creates a ton of noise. Don't forget, when you defeat an enemy, you can collect the weapons and resources (wood, stone, and metal) they leave behind. Defeating two or three enemies during a match will typically allow you to collect more than enough resources, without having to do too much harvesting yourself.

If you see a weakness in a tall structure, and you know an enemy is at or near the top of it, shoot at that weak point. Making the structure collapse will cause your enemy to fall. A short fall will have little impact, but a fall from four (or more) levels up could be devastating.

Learn to Quickly Build "1x1" Fortresses

A 1x1 fortress is simply four walls around you, with a ramp in the center. It goes up multiple levels. Using wood allows you to build with the greatest speed, but using metal offers the greatest protection. Keep practicing until you're able to build this type of fortress very quickly, without having to think too much about it.

Here's how to build a 1x1 fortress:

First build one floor tile if the ground is uneven.

Next, build four vertical walls so they surround you.

In the center of the structure, build a ramp. As the ramp is being constructed, jump on it. You've now built one level of a 1x1 fortress. Repeat these steps until the fortress has reached the desired height.

At the top, consider adding pyramid-shaped roof pieces around the roof for added protection when you peek out. However, if you need protection from above as well, add a flat roof and then a pyramid-shaped roof piece directly over your head.

This is a 1x1 fortress that's three levels tall. Using Edit mode, a window was added on the third level.

Learning to edit quickly, to add windows, doors, and other customizations to a structure you've built is an important skill to master. It takes practice to be able to edit structures at lightning-fast speed. When you're editing a wall tile, choose which of the nine squares you want to remove.

Removing one square creates a window. Removing two squares (one on top of the other) creates a door. Removing two squares next to each other creates an extra wide window.

While in Edit mode, edit a floor or ceiling tile to create a hole that you can easily travel through to climb up or down a level within the structure you're building.

SECTION 5
SURVIVAL STRATEGIES AND FIGHTING TIPS

Starting when you land on the island, there are a ton of strategies you should use to help you stay alive longer, so you can make it into the End Game.

Adapt Your Approach as Needed

No two matches are ever the same. Thus, it's important to adapt your strategy based on the location you're in and the challenges you're facing at any given moment. Making intelligent decisions, and then reacting instantly, will help you stay alive even during the most difficult and intense battles.

Anytime you're out in the open and need to travel between locations, run (don't walk) in a zig-zag pattern and keep jumping so that you don't become an easy-to-hit target.

Whenever you come across a Chug Jug, grab it, but unless your heath and shields are dangerously low, save it for when you really need it. As you enter the End Game and know you're about to encounter multiple enemies, this is a good time to replenish your health and shields to their maximum levels. A Chug Jug will fully replenish your health and shields, but it takes a full 15 seconds to consume, during which time you're defenseless, since you can't move or use a weapon. Make sure you're in a safe place before consuming or using a health and/or shield powerup item.

Immediately after a particularly rough firefight, as soon as it's safe, surround yourself with walls and consume or use a Med Kit, Bandages, or a Chug Jug, for example, in order to boost your health. If someone attacks you when your health is dangerously low, you'll wind up being defeated with just one bullet hit, especially if you have no shields. During the End Game, this soldier's health was at just 23 (out of 100), and there were still seven other enemies that could attack at any time.

Anytime you see someone quickly building a ramp that's more than three levels tall, wait for the ramp to reach a decent height (as the enemy soldier runs upward), and then use a submachine gun, drum gun, or any gun with a fast fire rate and large magazine, to aim at the bottom or midsection of the ramp. You should be able to destroy it within a few seconds (with multiple direct bullet hits or with an explosive weapon). Doing this will send your enemy plummeting to their demise. Remember, a wooden ramp tile only offers 190 HP worth of protection (after it's fully built), so shooting through it should be easy, even from a distance. If the tile isn't fully built when you attack it, it'll be even easier to destroy.

If you approach a house or building and the front door is already open, this could mean an enemy is still inside (and could ambush you), or that the structure has already been looted and everything worth collecting is now gone. Proceed inside with caution and be prepared for a firefight, especially if you hear footsteps or movement coming from inside. (Shown here on an iPad Pro.)

Before entering into a home or building you think might already be occupied, tiptoe up to a window and peak inside. If you see movement, shoot at enemies through the window. You'll likely catch them by surprise. (Shown here on an iPad Pro.)

Another option, if you suspect someone is already inside a building, is to toss Grenades, for example, through the window. Here, the soldier is about to toss three Stink Bombs through the window in order to smoke out and harm the enemies inside. (Shown here on an iPad Pro.)

Whenever you discover a house with a cellar door on the outside, smash open these doors with a pickaxe (or shoot the door to destroy it), and then head into the basement. You'll almost always find a chest, or at least one or two powerful weapons, along with some ammo. The basement you enter using the cellar door typically does not connect to the rest of the house, so you may need to exit the basement and then enter through the front or back door of the house in order to explore the rest of the house. (Shown here on an iPad Pro.)

At any given time, your soldier can harvest or collect and then carry up to 1,000 wood, 1,000 stone, and 1,000 metal. Anytime you're traveling between locations, for example, take the time to harvest resources. Smashing wooden pallets with a pickaxe will generate more wood than an average tree. You'll often find wooden pallets in and around buildings. An abundance of large and extra-thick trees (which also generate wood) can be found in and around Wailing Woods, as well as in between points of interest. (Shown here on an iPad Pro.)

Just after the storm expands, if you're near the border, stay on the safe side, hide behind something, and be ready to shoot at enemies as they exit the storm-ravaged area. Anytime you encounter a vehicle, it can serve as a shield if you crouch down behind it when you're under attack. When no enemies are around, any type of vehicle can also be smashed with a pickaxe in order to harvest and collect metal. (Shown here on an iPad Pro.)

Anytime your shields are low (or in this case at zero), drink a Shield Potion to replenish your Shield meter by 50 (up to 100). This soldier was out in the open when she drank the Shield Potion. This was not a smart strategy, because for about five seconds while this item was being consumed, she was defenseless. An enemy could easily have shot her from any distance and eliminated her from the match. In this situation, it would have been much smarter to build four walls around the soldier before consuming the Shield Potion.

If you need to boost your resources, go into any house or building and start smashing things with your pickaxe. Within a home, smashing the furniture and walls, for example, will generate wood. Smashing the appliances will generate metal. Smashing the stone fireplace (when there is one) will generate stone. Another way to build up resources, but that requires more risk, is to engage enemies in battle. Anytime you defeat an enemy soldier, you're able to grab any of the weapons, ammo, loot items, and resources they were carrying before they got eliminated from the match. So, if the enemy was carrying 500 wood, 800 stone, and 600 metal, grab the resource icons you discover where the enemy was defeated, and those resources become yours.

When playing the Duos or Squads game play mode, you're able to share weapons, ammo, loot items, and resources with your squad members. To share resources when one of your teammates is standing near you, access your Backpack Inventory screen. Select the resource you want to share (wood, stone, or metal), and then select the Drop option. From this pop-up slider, determine how much of the selected resource you're holding that you want to share. Select the Drop option again and allow your teammate to pick up the resource icon from the ground. (Shown here on an iPad Pro.)

A sniper rifle with a scope allows you to really zoom in and target your enemies from a distance. When you have a rifle with a thermal scope, you're able to zoom in and see your enemies from a distance, even when they're hiding behind something or within a fortress. From outdoors, a thermal scope can also show you the glow of a chest that's hidden within a building. Once you notice an enemy is hiding behind something, instead of wasting rifle bullets, use a long-range projectile weapon, such as a Rocket Launcher, to destroy the entire structure your enemy is hiding in. This strategy will help you conserve ammo and potentially defeat more enemies, especially during the End Game. When your enemies are clustered close together, they're easier to defeat (or at least injure) when you blast them with an explosive weapon.

During firefights it's almost always to your advantage to be higher up than your opponent, so that you're shooting downward at your target. There are several ways to achieve this. For example, you can build a ramp, stand on a pre-existing object, or in this case, climb to a higher level of a building or mountain and then snipe at enemies below.

Refer back to the screenshot on the right, found on the previous page. A firefight took place during an End Game. There were three enemies remaining, and one was hiding inside the wooden fortress below his enemy. The soldier who had the height advantage bombarded the roof of the lower fortress with gunfire until it was destroyed and the enemy hiding was defeated.

Port-A-Forts are rare, but if you've found one and you're carrying it, activate it if you get caught in a surprise attack and need instant protection.

Quickly get to the top of the fort by jumping on the tires.

Immediately build a metal floor piece to block the entrance to the fort's upper area. This will prevent enemies from entering the fort and sneaking up on you.

For added protection, build a metal pyramid-shaped tile over the floor tile you just built, and then peek over the top edge of the fort and shoot at your enemies below.

To counter when an enemy creates a Port-A-Fort, as soon as you see this happening, quickly build a ramp that points directly toward the fort as it's being built, get to a higher level than the fort, and then jump down into it. If you can do this before or at the same time your enemy reaches the top of the Port-A-Fort they just built, you'll be in a great position to defeat them with your most powerful short-range weapon. You can also just shoot them from above, since a Port-A-Fort has no roof.

In this situation, an enemy created a basic fortress with four stone and wood walls around him to offer a fair level of protection. The fact that several different resources were used for such a small shelter could indicate that the soldier hiding inside is low on resources. What's missing from this structure is a roof. This shelter can easily be spotted through the scope of a sniper rifle. At this point, the enemy holding the rifle has several choices.

One option is for the soldier holding the sniper rifle to wait for his enemy to peek their head over the top of the fortress. He can then use the sniper rifle to pick off his enemy with a headshot.

Another option would be to use a Rocket Launcher and aim for the inside of this small fortress (through the exposed top), so that the explosion defeats whoever is inside. A third option would be to sneak up closer and then toss a few Grenades or explosive weapons directly into this fortress. This is the riskiest option, but it can work well if you move fast.

At the start of a match, instead of leaping from the Battle Bus and landing in the middle of a popular point of interest that you know will be populated by a bunch of enemy soldiers, consider landing on the outskirts and collecting weapons, ammo, loot items, and resources first, and then traveling to the desired point of interest. Not only will you be better prepared to engage in battle, but the enemy soldiers who have already been there for a few minutes will have defeated some of the other soldiers by the time you get there, so you'll encounter fewer enemies. The hut that's located at the top-left (which often contains a chest in its loft) can be found on a hill just outside of Tilted Towers (near map coordinates D6).

After collecting weapons, ammo, and potentially loot items, as well as resources, from this small hut, slide down the cliff and directly enter Tilted Towers. You'll save time if you land directly on this hut's roof and smash through it to discover what's in the loft and on the floor on the main level.

Every point of interest has at least one structure on its outskirts that contains weapons, ammo, loot items, and/or resources you can use to build up your arsenal. The bottom screenshot above shows a decrepit house that can be found outside Paradise Palms, near the border between the green area of the island and the desert.

Whether you're in a match alone in Solo mode, or you're working with teammates in a Duos or Squads game, a Cozy Campfire offers a way to replenish your soldier's health after a battle. Multiple soldiers can heal at the same time by standing close to the fire. Plus, if you pile two Cozy Campfires on top of each other, you can reap twice the healing benefit.

Because it takes 30 seconds to discover the full healing benefits of a Cozy Campfire, make sure you're in a safe and secluded place when you activate it. Build walls around yourself for added protection. If multiple soldiers are standing close to the fire, have one person stand guard with their weapon drawn. Remember, any time you use a health or shields powerup, you can't use a weapon at the same time and your soldier needs to be standing still. He or she is vulnerable to attack.

Throughout the island are many small huts. Inside, you'll sometimes find weapons, ammo, loot items, or resource icons lying on the ground, although sometimes they're empty. You can use these structures to hide in while you rest or replenish your health and shields using powerups. Another option is to hide inside and ambush an enemy when he or she opens the door and comes looking for you. You could also booby trap the inside of the cabin using a Trap or Remote Explosives, for example, and then leave (closing the door behind you). When the enemy enters, they'll go boom.

There are many houses scattered throughout the island—not just within labeled points of interest on the map. If there's a chest to be found inside, it'll often be located in the attic, basement, or garage. In the various rooms, you'll often discover weapons, ammo, loot items, and resource icons lying out in the open waiting to be grabbed (if you're the first soldier to search the house).

From outside, listen carefully for enemy movement as you approach and enter any house, building, or structure. If you hear movement and don't want to fight at the moment, consider moving on without entering that structure. If you do decide to enter, go in with your weapon drawn and be ready for an ambush. While you're searching the house, feel free to smash everything inside to collect resources.

As you make your way between points of interest on the island and attempt to stay clear of the storm, you'll discover many hills and mountains. Never leap off of a cliff, or you'll wind up injured or worse. Instead, slide down the edge of the cliff and you'll land on the ground safely, with no loss of HP.

When you encounter silos (like these two) in a farming area, or a metal water tower in one of the suburban areas, use your pickaxe to smash them. Inside, you'll often (but not always) discover a chest. You'll also harvest some metal.

You can't smash or destroy piles of tires, but you can jump on them to reach a higher altitude. If the tires are near the side of a building or structure, you can often jump on the tires and reach the roof with one leap.

Several locations on the island contain junkyards, where you'll find piles of crushed vehicles that create a maze-like area when you're at ground level. There's often useful loot to be collected on the ground, but you need to watch out for enemies who may be lurking around every turn. Plus, there's always a threat from enemy snipers above you.

To stay safe, avoid the ground level of these congested, maze-like areas until you know they're clear of enemies. The best way to accomplish this is to build a ramp and climb to the top of the tallest pile, or to go to a higher level in a building that surrounds the junkyard and shoot at enemies you spot below. Remember you always want a height advantage, if possible.

When you're playing a Duos or Squads game and you get injured, all you can do is crawl around. You can't build, fight, or use any of your loot items. At this point, hope one of your teammates will come to your rescue and revive you. While you're waiting, whenever possible, crawl to somewhere safe. Hopefully, the enemy won't approach and finish you off before help arrives.

While you're being revived, both the injured soldier and the teammate who is doing the healing become vulnerable to attack, since neither can move or use a weapon during the revive process. Thus, you definitely want to revive someone only when it's safe to do so.

Don't forget, as long as you have resources, you're able to build almost anywhere on the island, including directly on top of existing structures (or within them). This wooden fortress was built on top of the structure located in the center of Pleasant Park. From the top of this fortress, you're able to see 360 degrees around you, so you can easily spot and then shoot at enemies.

Anytime you build a structure, think about how it will protect you, but also consider the location and choose a building spot that offers the best vantage point from which to launch attacks.

It's often easier to reach the attic of a house if you get to the roof from the outside and then smash your way downward. You can do this by landing on a roof (after exiting the Battle Bus) or by building a ramp outside that goes from ground level directly to the roof.

The fastest way to travel across a large body of water, such as the lake in Loot Lake, is to build a wooden bridge over the water and run across it. You can just walk through the water, but this is a slow process. Anytime you're out in the open, you're exposed to potential attacks. Here, an enemy soldier can be hiding with a sniper rifle from anywhere along the edge of the lake and shoot at you as you cross. Be prepared to quickly build vertical walls to protect you from incoming bullets. As you cross the bridge, run in a zigzag pattern and keep jumping to make yourself a fast-moving and difficult target to hit.

When it comes to protecting yourself from incoming bullets, never underestimate the usefulness of a single metal pyramid-shaped tile. Each can withstand between 140 HP and 460 HP worth of damage (based on what it's made from). These are easy to build. Just crouch down and hide behind it. Anytime you build with metal, keep in mind that until the tile is fully built it does not offer full protection. If you need instant protection, build with wood first, and then reinforce your structure with metal.

Instead of hiding behind a pyramid-shaped tile, you can crouch down and build one directly on top of yourself. This too offers protection. For even more protection, if you have time, first build four walls to surround yourself, add a pyramid-shaped roof to the structure, and then build another pyramid-shaped tile to hide under within the fort.

Remote Explosives offer a great way to booby trap an object or struc-ture. Figure out where you want to place these explosives and then go hide. Wait for an enemy to approach, and then detonate the explosives. Make sure you're far enough away to avoid the impact of the explosion, but that you have a good line of sight to the boobytrapped area, so you know when to set off the explosion. In this case, the door to a house's basement was boobytrapped using multiple Remote Explosives.

Once Remote Explosives are placed and activated, they emit a flashing blue light. Take this into account and try to hide the explosives from view when you place them. Now move away from the explosives.

As you can see, the explosion from three Remote Explosives gutted the entire basement and most of the house's first floor. If enemies had been in the house, they would have been injured or eliminated from the match instantly. Remember, as you're exploring the island, if you notice flashing blue lights, stay away, or you could be the one about to get caught in an explosion.

Vending Machines are randomly scattered throughout the island. Using resources (wood, stone, or metal), you're able to purchase rare and powerful weapons and/or loot items. These machines offer a great way to boost your arsenal. However, making purchases will quickly diminish your resources. To protect yourself when making a purchase, consider building walls around yourself and the Vending Machine.

Instead of making a purchase, hide near a Vending Machine with your gun drawn. Wait for an enemy soldier to approach the machine and make a purchase, and then launch a surprise attack. When you defeat that enemy, you'll be able to collect everything he or she was carrying, including whatever was just purchased from the Vending Machine.

Points of interest like Shifty Shafts are fun to explore, because the underground tunnels contain lots of useful weapons, ammo, loot items, and resources to collect. As you explore these tunnels, you can't see anything around the turns, so listen carefully for the movement of your enemies, and as you travel through the tunnels, crouch down and tip-toe, so you make the least amount of noise possible. Always keep your weapon drawn and ready to fire as you go around turns.

While in the underground tunnels of places like Shifty Shafts, listen carefully for the sound of chests. You'll often find them hidden behind walls that you need to smash through in order to reach them. Sometimes, you can also see the glow of the chests from between the wood plank walls.

As you travel in between points of interest, you'll sometimes come across red Apples or blue Mushrooms on the ground. When you pick up and consume an Apple, your Health meter gets a 5HP boost (up to a maximum of 100). When you consume a Mushroom, your Shield meter gets a 5HP boost (up to a maximum of 100). You can't pick up and collect these powerups, store them in your backpack, and then use them when you need them. Instead, you must consume these items when and where you discover them.

From the Item Shop, you can purchase a vast selection of outfits to customize the appearance of your soldier. It's assumed that the gamers who showcase the rarest, "legendary," and most elaborate outfits, with a separate pickaxe design and backpack design, are the best, most experienced players.

If you get really good playing *Fortnite: Battle Royale,* forego the fancy outfits and dress your soldier in the default (free) outfit, use the default pickaxe, and don't add back bling. This way, your adversaries will often assume you're a noob and pay less attention to you in the game.

After stepping into a Rift, you'll be catapulted into the sky and able to glide back toward land using your glider. While airborne, you can cover a lot of territory. The drawback is that while you're using your glider and still in the air, enemy soldiers can shoot at you from the ground and you're basically defenseless. Try to avoid flying over heavily populated areas. Rifts-to-Go loot items can be collected and used anywhere.

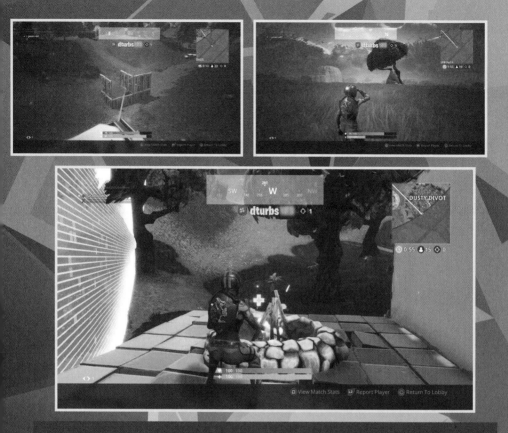

When you're caught in the storm running toward the safe area of the island, participating in a firefight is seldom a smart strategy. If you decide to confront an enemy while in the storm, make sure your Health meter is maxed out when you start. Try to finish the battle quickly, and then use a Bouncer, Launch Pad, Shopping Kart, or ideally an ATK to help you escape the storm faster. Stepping into a Rift can also be helpful when it comes to making a quick exit from your current location.

While still in the storm, you can replenish some health HP by consuming or using a powerup, but this often takes time. If you wait too long to use it, you'll be burning away your health at the same time you're replenishing it, and you'll wind up stuck in the storm and perishing with zero health. If you use a health powerup while in the storm, your Health meter should still be at 40 or higher.

As soon as you exit the storm, find a safe place to hide, and then use a Cozy Campfire or a Med Kit, for example, to fully replenish your Health meter before moving on to your next challenge or battle.

Shooting at the bottom or mid-section of a tall ramp will cause it to come crashing down, and whoever is standing on it will likely be injured or perish from the fall.

These "No Dancing" signs are scattered around the island. When you see one, you're going to want to dance. Your enemies will too! Find a nearby place to hide that's in line of sight to the sign. Wait for one of your enemies to approach the sign and start dancing, then shoot him. While a soldier is dancing, he can't use a weapon or build, so for a few seconds he's vulnerable to attack. Make one successful headshot, and the enemy will be history.

Lazy Links tends to be a popular area on the island. Instead of landing in the heart of it, stay in the outskirts. Within the golf course's sand traps, you'll often find weapons, ammo, and/or loot items if you're the first soldier to get there.

If you're riding in an ATK alone, you can't drive and use a weapon at the same time, but you can run over enemies and smash through certain objects. Keep in mind, enemies can shoot at the ATK while it's moving, so drive fast and in a zigzag pattern to avoid getting hit. If you're trying to shoot at someone else driving an ATK, using a projectile weapon, such as a Rocket Launcher, is easier than trying to make a direct hit on a fast-moving target with a gun.

ATKs truly are all-terrain vehicles. In fact, they can go airborne if you drive over a jump or directly into a Rift. Shown here is an ATK in a Rift. When you land, you won't take damage from the Rift, and you could potentially cover a lot of territory. With practice, when an ATK is on land, you can leap out of it at any time and immediately begin shooting your weapon.

One of the most perfect places to land if you're looking for a spot that's secluded, away from the popular points of interest, and that's chock full of weapons, ammo, loot items, and resources, is the roof of this house that already has a wooden tower built on top of it. You'll find it by the coastline outside of Wailing Woods (between map coordinates I2.5 and J2.5). Once you've collected everything you need from this house, check its garage. Sometimes there's an ATK parked inside. If not, start running toward Wailing Woods, and harvest wood from the trees along the way. Pay attention to the direction the storm is moving and then decide where to go next.

SECTION 6

WELCOME TO THE END GAME: SURVIVAL AND COMBAT STRATEGIES

The goal of most *Fortnite: Battle Royale* players is to make it into the End Game during each match they play. If you want to survive until you enter into the Final Circle, and ultimately win matches, you'll need to start preparing early in the match.

The longer you wait during each match to collect resources and the right combination of loot items and weapons, for example, the more risk you're taking. Your chance of encountering enemies increases as the eye of the storm shrinks.

Preparing for the End Game

Not every end game requires a soldier to build an elaborate fortress in order to win. It's more important to go into the End Game with the best possible collection of weapons, have plenty of ammunition for those weapons, and to have an abundance of resources collected so you can build ramps, protective structures, and fortresses as they're needed, based on the challenges you encounter.

Try to go into every End Game with up to 1,000 wood, 1,000 stone, and 1,000 metal. Having plenty of wood is the most important for quickly building ramps and protective walls. Being able to build a fortress from metal ensures it'll be able to withstand more damage from attacks. A Port-A-Fort can be very useful during an End Game. It offers protection yet requires no resources until you build extensions onto it or modify it.

Along with having adequate levels of resources, make sure that within your backpack's inventory, you have the loot items and weapons you'll need to launch attacks (such as a weapon with a scope and a projectile explosive weapon).

About halfway through each match, start thinking about the End Game and preparing for it. By defeating enemies in the later stages of a match, but prior to the End Game, you're able to grab all of the weapons, ammo, loot items, and resources that they've collected. This is a great way to build your arsenal and ensure you go into the End Game nicely equipped with resources.

As the End Game approaches, within your backpack, you ideally want to have:

- At least one sniper rifle with a scope (or thermal scope).
- At least one projectile weapon that shoots explosives, such as a Rocket Launcher or Grenade Launcher.
- One or two Med Kits, Chug Jugs, or Bandages, so you can replenish your health. A Cozy Campfire is useful, but only if you can spare 30 seconds for it to fully work. Go into the End Game with your Health meter and Shield meter at 100.
- One or two Shield Potions to replenish your soldier's shields after each firefight. You can use one less slot in your backpack if you carry one or more Chug Jug or Slurp Juice consumables that simultaneously replenishes your soldier's health and shields.
- At least one short-range weapon and one mid-range weapon, since you'll likely need to engage in a firefight either out in the open, within your own fortress, or when you invade an enemy's fortress.
- Make sure you have plenty of ammo on hand for each type of weapon you're bringing with you into the End Game. You can sometimes collect additional weapons and ammo from defeated enemies, but it's not always safe to do this.

Twelve End-Game Strategies to Get You Started

Here are twelve additional End-Game strategies that'll help you win:

1. If you're going to build a mighty fortress during the End Game, choose the best location to build it. This will likely be where you'll make your final stand in battle. Keep in mind, if you're in the dead-center of the Final Circle, you will become the center of attention, which probably isn't good.

2. Make sure your fortress is tall, well-fortified, and that it offers an excellent, 360-degree view of the surrounding area from the top level.

3. If your fortress gets destroyed, be prepared to move quick, and have a backup strategy in place that will help to ensure your survival. Having the element of surprise for your attacks gives you a tactical advantage. Don't become an easy target to hit. Keep moving around your fort, or while you're out in the open!

4. During the End Game, don't engage every remaining player. Allow them to fight amongst themselves to reduce their numbers, plus reduce or even deplete their ammo and resources.

5. Only rely on a sniper rifle (or scoped rifle) to make long-range shots if you have really good aim and a clear line of sight to your enemy. Otherwise use explosive weapons that'll cause damage over a wide area. A Rocket Launcher, for example, is ideal. This type of weapon will damage or destroy an enemy fortress, plus injure or defeat an enemy soldier who is inside.

6. Always keep tabs on the location of your remaining enemies during the End Game. Don't allow them to sneak up behind you, for example. If you lose track of an enemy who you know is nearby, listen carefully for their movement.

7. Don't invest a lot of resources into a massive and highly fortified fortress until you know you're in the Final Circle during a match. Refer to the map and the displayed timer. Otherwise, when the storm expands and moves, you could

find it necessary to abandon your fort, and then need to build another one quickly, in a not-so-ideal location. Having to rebuild will use up your resources.

8. Base pushers are enemies that aren't afraid to leave their fortress and attempt to attack yours during the final minutes of a match. Be prepared to deal with their close-range threat. Thanks to tweaks made to the game, it's no longer necessary to build an elaborate fortress to win a match.

9. If two or three enemies remain, focus on one at a time. Determine who appears to be the most imminent and largest threat. Be prepared to change priorities at a moment's notice, based on the actions of your enemies.

10. Some final battles take place on ramps, not from within fortresses. In this situation, use speed and quick reflexes to get higher up than your enemy. At this point, having accurate aim with the proper weapon is the key to winning. Try to destroy the bottom of an enemy's ramp to make the whole thing come crashing down. The soldier standing on the ramp will be injured or defeated, based on how far he or she falls to the ground.

11. Have a Chug Jug on hand to replenish your health and shields if you're attacked and incur damage, but are not defeated. Make sure you're well protected when you drink the Chug Jug. Med Kits are also great for maintaining HP during End Games.

12. Study the live streams created by expert *Fortnite* players (on YouTube and Twitch.tv) to learn their End-Game strategies and see how they react to various challenges.

Additional End-Game Strategies

The following are some additional strategies you can use during an End Game to improve your chances of survival. Remember, once you know what needs to be done, you'll still need to practice your building techniques and perfect your aiming skills using a variety of different weapons.

In between firefights, get somewhere safe and replenish your health and shields.

After defeating an enemy, don't run up to grab what they've left behind, unless you know it's safe. During the end game, focus on quickly grabbing resources and health/shield powerups, along with any weapons you know will be useful during the final minutes of a match.

If you plan to rush an enemy fortress during a Duos or Squads match, have one of your teammates stay behind with a long-range weapon and provide cover fire as you approach. As you approach, start throwing Grenades or other explosive weapons to cause as much damage and disruption as possible—before you actually reach your destination and start shooting.

Once you're in the Final Circle, build up your fortress and try to maintain a height advantage over your opponents.

You can build an elaborate fortress, but if its base or mid-section is not sturdy, an enemy soldier will come along and shoot at the weak spots, causing the entire fortress to collapse with you in it.

As you're building a 1x1 fortress, consider adding a Trap to one of the walls as an added layer of protection against enemy intruders.

If you're playing with squad members, don't gather close together within your base. One well-aimed explosive projectile weapon launched by an opponent could take out the entire squad with a single shot.

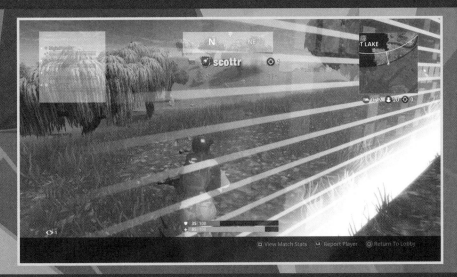

Staying close to the storm's edge could provide some level of protection, but stay ahead of its movement. Always be prepared for an enemy to purposely go into the storm and reposition themselves behind you, so he/she can launch a surprise attack from behind when your attention is on the action happening in front of you. Here, the soldier is on the safe side of the storm, but just barely.

Study the terrain carefully. If you notice there's a lot of unusable or open terrain, try to anticipate the best location to establish your fortress, preferably at the top of a mountain or hill, so you have a natural height advantage. By looking at the Location Map, you can see that in addition to a lot of flat and open land, a portion of the circle covers the lake area. Within open water is never where you want to be—especially during the End Game.

If you need to travel a good distance in order to stay within the circle, use a Launch Pad or Booster to catapult you into the sky, and then navigate your glider to the desired landing location. Consider placing a Launch Pad or Booster within your fortress and then step on it to catapult into the air to obtain a good view of your surroundings and potentially locate your enemies. Just make sure you land back in your fortress. Doing this will reveal your location if enemies are paying attention. You can also use a Launch Pad or Booster within your fortress to make a quick getaway and quickly move to another area of the circle.

If time permits, climb to the top of the tallest hill or mountain to gain a height advantage within the circle. Just be careful about wasting resources you may need to build a fortress with during the next skirmish.

The squad of enemies this soldier is fighting are at a disadvantage because they were hiding behind haystacks. As soon as their cover was blown, they were vulnerable to attack. A haystack offers no protection whatsoever.

During this End Game, the pictured soldier has two of his own squad mates by his side. Two enemy soldiers remained in the match, and the only visible fortress seen off in the distance was empty. This soldier used his sniper rifle's scope to target all of the bushes where he figured out the remaining enemy soldiers were hiding. He then picked them off one at a time from the safety of his fortress.

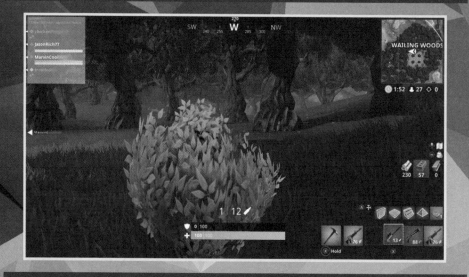

If you choose to wear a Bush item as camouflage, your soldier will look ridiculous if he or she starts moving around. A moving Bush attracts attention. The best use of this item is if you stay perfectly still to blend in with other bushes and trees around you. A Bush offers no protection against an enemy attack. One direct hit from a weapon, and the Bush disappears and leaves you fully visible. While hiding in a Bush, you can shoot a weapon, so if an enemy comes close, you'll potentially have the element of surprise if you start shooting.

This soldier has chosen to skip building a fortress, and spent the End Game moving around on foot, defeating one enemy at a time using a combination of a sniper rifle with a thermal scope and a Rocket Launcher. Luckily, he stocked up on plenty of ammo for both of these long-range weapons. Here, only one enemy remains, but this soldier (who is hiding under a tree and out of sight) does not know where his enemy is hiding.

The soldier soon found his one remaining enemy hiding out in a tall 1x1 fortress on a hill. The opponent had the height advantage in the firefight that followed, which ultimately allowed the opponent to win the match.

Instead of building one elaborate fortress during the End Game, this soldier ran around, primarily with a Rocket Launcher in hand, and blew away one enemy fortress and the enemy within each fortress at a time. This is a relatively easy task when the opposing fortresses are made of wood. This strategy worked because throughout the match, this player stocked up on the Rocket ammo needed for a Rocket Launcher.

During the End Game, you'll sometimes spot Supply Drops falling from the sky. Approaching and opening one, however, can be risky if it's out in the open and you know you're surrounded by a handful of skilled enemy soldiers. If you decide to approach the Supply Drop, quickly build walls around it before opening it. The payoff could be worthwhile if you're able to grab a stockpile of resources and ammo, along with one or two "Legendary" weapons.

This soldier has a height advantage during the End Game, as well as a fortress made mainly from stone. His problem was a lack of powerful long-range weapons. As a result, he had to leave the safety of his own base and rush his opponent's base and engage in a close-range firefight to better accommodate the weapons in his arsenal.

SECTION 7
FORTNITE: BATTLE ROYALE RESOURCES

There are two proven ways to become an awesome *Fortnite: Battle Royale* player. First, learn everything you can about the game and study how other expert players compete. Next, practice. When it comes to watching other players, four popular options include:

1. Instead of leaving a match after you've been eliminated, stick around and watch the rest of each match in Spectator mode before returning to the Lobby.
2. Watch pre-recorded YouTube videos produced by expert gamers that offer tips and advice, as well as detailed instruction. Just make sure the video applies to the most recent version of the game.
3. Watch the live streams of highly ranked *Fortnite: Battle Royale* players on a service like YouTube Live or Twitch.tv.
4. If Playground mode is active within the game (this is a feature that Epic Games periodically shuts down), spend time there exploring the island at your own pace without having to deal with the storm. Practice your building skills, learn all about the different terrain types on the island, and participate in mock fights with friends—without having to worry about being eliminated from a match.

On YouTube (www.youtube.com), Facebook Watch (www.Facebook.com/Watch), or Twitch.TV (www.twitch.tv/directory/game/Fortnite), in the Search field, enter the search phrase "*Fortnite: Battle Royale*" to discover many game-related channels, live streams, and pre-recorded videos.

Also, be sure to check out these awesome online resources that will help you become a better *Fortnite: Battle Royale* player:

WEBSITE OR YOUTUBE CHANNEL NAME	DESCRIPTION	URL
Fandom's *Fortnite* Wiki	Discover the latest news and strategies related to *Fortnite: Battle Royale*.	http://fortnite.wikia.com/wiki/Fortnite_Wiki
FantasticalGamer	A popular YouTuber who publishes *Fortnite* tutorial videos.	www.youtube.com/user/FantasticalGamer
FBR Insider	The *Fortnite: Battle Royale Insider* website offers game-related news, tips, and strategy videos.	www.fortniteinsider.com
Fortnite Gamepedia Wiki	Read up-to-date descriptions of every weapon, loot item, and ammo type available within *Fortnite: Battle Royale*. This Wiki also maintains a comprehensive database of soldier outfits and related items released by Epic Games.	https://fortnite.gamepedia.com/Fortnite_Wiki
Fortnite Intel	An independent source of news related to *Fortnite: Battle Royale*.	www.fortniteintel.com
Fortnite Scout	Check your personal player stats, and analyze your performance using a bunch of colorful graphs and charts. Also check out the stats of other *Fortnite: Battle Royale* players.	www.fortnitescout.com
Fortnite Stats & Leaderboard	This is an independent website that allows you to view your own *Fortnite*-related stats or discover the stats from the best players in the world.	https://fortnitestats.com
Game Informer Magazine's *Fortnite* Coverage	Discover articles, reviews, and news about *Fortnite: Battle Royale* published by *Game Informer* magazine.	www.gameinformer.com/search/searchresults.aspx?q=Fortnite
Game Skinny Online Guides	A collection of topic-specific strategy guides related to *Fortnite*.	www.gameskinny.com/tag/fortnite-guides/

GameSpot's *Fortnite* Coverage	Check out the news, reviews, and game coverage related to *Fortnite: Battle Royale* that's been published by GameSpot.	www.gamespot.com/fortnite
IGN Entertainment's *Fortnite* Coverage	Check out all IGN's past and current coverage of *Fortnite*.	www.ign.com/wikis/fortnite
Jason R. Rich's Website and Social Media Feeds	Share your *Fortnite: Battle Royale* game play strategies with this book's author and learn about his other books.	www.JasonRich.com www.FortniteGameBooks.com Twitter: @JasonRich7 Instagram: @JasonRich7
Microsoft's Xbox One *Fortnite* Website	Learn about and acquire *Fortnite: Battle Royale* if you're an Xbox One gamer.	www.microsoft.com/en-US/store/p/Fortnite-Battle-Royalee/BT5P2X999VH2
MonsterDface YouTube and Twitch.tv Channels	Watch video tutorials and live game streams from an expert *Fortnite* player.	www.youtube.com/user/MonsterdfaceLive www.Twitch.tv/MonsterDface
Ninja	Check out the live and recorded game streams from Ninja, one of the most highly skilled *Fortnite: Battle Royale* players in the world on Twitch.tv and YouTube.	www.twitch.tv/ninja_fortnite_hyper www.youtube.com/user/NinjasHyper
Nomxs	A YouTube and Twitch.tv channel hosted by online personality Simon Britton (Nomxs). He too is one of *Fortnite*'s top-ranked players.	https://youtu.be/np-8cmsUZmc or www.twitch.tv/videos/259245155
Official Epic Games YouTube Channel for *Fortnite: Battle Royale*	The official *Fortnite: Battle Royale* YouTube channel.	www.youtube.com/user/epicfortnite

Your Fortnite: Battle Royale Adventure Continues . . .

Epic Games does not want anyone getting bored playing *Fortnite: Battle Royale*, which is why the game is updated every week or two. It's with each new gaming Season, however, that a loose storyline unfolds, and major updates and additions are made to virtually all aspects of the gaming experience.

Whether you enjoy playing alone against 99 adversaries in Solo mode, or prefer to team up with online friends when you experience the Duos or Squads mode, you'll quickly discover that each and every *Fortnite: Battle Royale* match you experience is challenging, fun, unique, and rather intense. Becoming an expert player will take time and a lot of practice, so don't worry if you're not winning matches right away.

Instead of focusing exclusively on winning matches and achieving #1 Victory Royale, take time to explore the island, engage in firefights using different selections of weapons, learn to become a master (and very fast) builder, try out using various loot items in new and creative ways, or hop into the driver's seat of an All Terrain Kart (ATK) and experience the thrill of racing around the island.

You'll develop the skill needed to win matches over time, so be patient. As you experience *Fortnite: Battle Royale*, the most important thing is to always have fun!